If i Can Help Somebody

By

Rev. Dr. Alvin Larke, Jr.

2023

IF i CAN HELP
SOMEBODY

REV. DR. ALVIN LARKE, JR.

DEDICATION

This Book is dedicated to Boston Johnson, II. Mr. Johnson epitomizes the all-in-one, the father, the teacher, mentor, and role model.

In memory of my mother and father, Staretha Aaron Larke and Alvin Larke Sr.

My maternal grandparents, Pennie Hudson Aaron and Hayward Aaron Sr.

My paternal grandparents, Henrietta Johnson Larke and Ned Mays

My devoted friend and wife, Dr. Patricia J. Larke

My biological children, Dr. Altricia Wilretha Larke and Aaron Reynard Larke

Siblings

Shirley Jean Larke Johnson

Emma Jane Larke Glover

Ruth Elaine Jefferies Massenburg

Dr. Charles Gibson. Larke

Johnnie Larke

George Howard Larke

Warren Larke

Dr. Teresa LaTrell Larke Pope

"Adopted Children"

Wash A. Jones

Jonathan Williams

Rodrick Moore

Sharon Goodwine Honor

Marcus Sodek

Wesley Bauerschlag

11 Grandchildren

15 Great-Grandchildren

TABLE OF CONTENTS

PREFACE

If I Can Help Somebody embodies the lives touched by so many, for so many. Grown folks. Preachers. Teachers. Custodians. Educated and not-so-educated. Common folks. Kinfolks. Black. White. Hispanic. Brazilian. Young and old. Saints and ain'ts. Church folks and non-church folks. You made a difference in my life, good or bad, but I took it for good, even though Satan wanted me to see it as evil.

I have been privileged to talk to many. I received so much from so many people. I am amazed as I write this and recall how my grandmothers, grandfathers, parents, aunts, uncles, siblings, cousins, wife, children, grandchildren, and great grandchildren have all impacted my life. My early recollections of "Boy, you are going be something," to the refrain of, "You will never amount to anything." As polarizing as these two statements are, they have stuck with me until this day in my pitfalls and successes.

As you read this manuscript, reflect on those individuals who have impacted your life, good or bad, and thank God for His goodness. And If You Can Help Somebody, please help. God will be pleased and so will *you*!

Be the Boston Johnson, who, because of him, you are, and I am.

IN THE BEGINNING

Picture of the house I grew up in

Staretha Aaron Larke was severely burned in November of 1946, as she stood with her back to the fireplace in a home rented from Mr. Johnny Tavelle. She was taken to a hospital in Charleston, South Carolina. She told me that story many times as we talked about why my other siblings perceived that I was her favorite child. Since third degree burns were on her back and her side, she had to lay on her stomach, and, therefore, was given a pill daily to quench her resulting labor pains.

She was discharged on the morning of December 17th. On the morning of Wednesday, December 18th, I was born. Mrs. Liddie

Roundtree, the community midwife, delivered me around 6 a.m. She also delivered the remainder of my five siblings. Since I was due in January of 1947, I was an eight-month infant, and the chances of survival were slim at that time. I was named after my father and nurtured by my mom for many years.

We lived and worked for Mr. Johnny as part of our rental agreement. We paid him $3.50 per month. On a couple occasions, I took the rent money in a tied-up handkerchief to Mr. Johnny. I was told to knock at the back door, and wait for him or his sister, Mrs. Alice, to come to the door and receive the money. No receipt, just thank you. Then I went back home!

As children we had to pick cotton and living on Mr. Johnny's place required us to pick his cotton first. We often thought that Mr. Johnny and Mrs. Alice couldn't talk because they would bow their heads as they passed in their car. We would ask Moma why? She said that was their way of acknowledging us. Wow, couldn't they just say hello?

My first job was to get water from the creek for Moma's washing. She washed every Wednesday. I would waste a lot of the water out of my bucket on my way from the spring. Moma boiled her water in iron pots in the backyard and then poured the water into two tubs, one for washing and one for rinsing. It was so nice that my mom always made me feel good, very good when I made an effort to do anything to assist her. Yes, I was beginning to earn the title, "a Moma's boy", a term that I treasured until she passed. I always tried to ask my mom, what I could do to make things better for her.

School years swiftly passed.

I found out I was going to school during the summer when I began picking cotton. I didn't mind picking cotton, but desired to talk and not bend my grizzle (back). I wasn't old enough to have a back. This particular day, I talked back to Mrs. Viola Roundtree who said that I was mannish because I hadn't been baptized as a child. We went to her house that day for lunch. She also lived on Mr. Johnny's place. During the lunch hour that day, she put me between her knees and baptized me in her home. That day, Mrs. Viola became my godmother, and she served graciously in that capacity until she passed in 1984. My mother said to me that I had to work in order to get money for school clothing. I would be entering first grade at the age of five. I was told to go, even though I was only five and would not be six until December 18th. In hindsight, I think my sister Emma had gone early as a companion to my older sister Shirley. I would be a boy, walking a little over two miles with my sisters.

Modern Day Picture of Kathwood Elementary School

We walked to the Kathwood School, a Rosenwald school for colored children during that time. It was a two-room school with one large heater used to heat both rooms. The first-through-fourth grades were in one room and the fifth-through-eighth in the adjacent room. The school was adjacent to the church all of us attended as children. We had to assist by putting wood in the heater. When I started school, I wasn't old enough to gather wood or put wood in the heater.

My truthfulness got me in trouble. On December 18th, I was happy as a lark and was asked by Mrs. Ford, why? I wasn't happy because it was our day to get out for the holidays, but because it was my sixth birthday. I was told not to return after the holidays, but I continued reading and practicing cursive writing by joining my letters together. While I advanced to the second grade when I returned the next year, my brother, Charles, started the first grade. Like me, he started school a year early.

During the Christmas holidays, riding on the handlebars of my Uncle Frank's bicycle, my left leg got caught in the spokes of the front tire. The x-ray revealed that my left leg was broken. A cast was placed on it from my thigh to my toes.

Walking the two miles to school with my crutches was horrible. I met Mrs. Quattlebaum, a teacher at the school, at the crossroad and rode to school with her. This lasted several months until I was able to change the cast and was eventually free of it. While my leg was broken, my first girlfriend carried my books for me. Her name was Shellie Ann.

We moved into our new house with running water that year. We also started riding a school bus to our new school, Sleepy Hollow Elementary School.

SLEEPY HOLLOW

Sleepy Hollow Elementary School circa 1954

We moved from Mr. Johnny's place during the summer of 1954 into a block, two-bedroom home with electricity, indoor plumbing, and running water. All six children shared a bedroom. We still had a wood stove in the kitchen and wood heater in our parent's room. We were happy for the running water, though we had to share the water. Usually, because I was the oldest boy, I took my bath first and then the boys followed after me. What I remember most about moving, was that my siblings (Shirley, Emma, Charles) and I had to move our gym set. We dragged the gym set from the old house to our new house.

When classes started in the fall, we had a new school with six classrooms and two indoor restrooms with one restroom for the boys and one restroom for the girls. Not only did we have restrooms at our new school, we also had a school bus that picked us up at the highway. It really beat walking the two and a half miles to and from Kathwood Elementary School. I was in third grade, Charles in second, Emma in fourth, and Shirley in the fifth. Since it was four of us, our lunch was eighty-eight cents each per week. Shirley worked in the kitchen that was a part of the cafeteria where we ate. Of the six teachers, Mr. Thomas was the principal and the only male. He taught sixth grade.

I continued to do well, making mostly A's with a few B's. My fourth-grade teacher, Miss Stephens, crushed my dreams the very first day of the school year. She asked each of us what we wanted to be when we grew up. When it was my time, I exclaimed that I wanted to be a preacher and a teacher. She said that it was impossible because of my speech impediment. I stuttered as a young child. Miss Stephens' remarks haunted me. I was upset for days and became very quiet in class. When my fourth-grade year came to a close, I was still thinking about what Miss Stephens had said to me.

All that summer, I was distraught because of Miss Stephens telling me what I couldn't become. It weighed heavily on me. Her words taught me how to pray. I learned how to pray in the cotton fields while taking my cow out in the mornings and returning her in the afternoon.

I attended Sunday School and church faithfully at St. Catherine CME Church. We (Shirley, Emma, Charles, and I) walked to Sunday School every Sunday. Our parents took us to church on the second Sunday because we only had worship on the second Sundays of each month. Daddy started taking us when he started attending and became an active member in the church. Mrs. Carrie Johnson was the superintendent. Mrs. Lucinda (Lucy) Williams taught elementary grades. Mrs. Mary Miller taught junior and high school students.

That summer really gave me a new revelation as to who I was called to be. It was a hot summer day; we were picking cotton for my Uncle Tug and Aunt Lillie. We had lunch break and returned later than usual. Moma asked me where we had been? I said, "to the bushes."

This was slang meaning we had gone to the restroom. They thought I was being truthful. Low and behold, I got sick and began to vomit. Up came the watermelon with all those black seeds. The truth, we boys had raided Mr. Marshall's watermelon patch. Mrs. Viola, my "godmother," told my Moma that I deserved a whipping. I got one that day in front of everyone. I was nine years old at the time, and I have never eaten watermelon since that day.

We had our Annual Summer Revival at St. Catherine the week leading up to the second Sunday in August. Several of us were sitting on the moaners bench. Emma, my sister, and my second cousin, Calvin, and I led the group. The moaners bench was the front pew used for unbelievers. At the age of nine, I sought the Lord because I felt a calling to be like Rev. N.G. Bryant, our neighbor, who was a preacher and teacher. Not only did Rev. Bryant have an excellent penmanship, but I wanted to have an excellent penmanship, too. I succeeded in getting the excellent penmanship and often had to write out information for my teachers.

I led the group that Wednesday night, August 8, 1956. Several of us, including my older sister, Emma, and second cousin Calvin joined church that night and were baptized on Sunday, August 12th. Rev. Seabrooks baptized us using the sprinkling method, practiced by the Methodist denomination. Grandma Hennie, our paternal grandmother, shouted that night as we accepted Christ. She was happy and they fanned her. Someone said, "Let her shout!" Needless to say, that was the last time she would shout and attend church. Grandma Hennie grew gravely ill and died on Saturday, September 15, 1956.

School began in the latter part of August, and I was in Mrs. Quattlebaum's class. I wondered if she would remember me from when she waited for me at the crossroad while I was on crutches in the second grade. She did remember me and was very cordial to me. I felt as if I was her "pet!" She asked the same question Miss Stephens asked years before. She asked what I desired to be when I grew up. I gave the same answer, but was hesitant.

Mrs. Quattlebaum confirmed that I could become whatever I desired to become. Wow! Happiness filled my heart and I felt my prayers had been answered. Someone confirmed that I could be a preacher and a teacher. She asked me to return to her classroom after eating my lunch. I worried about what others would think, but decided to return to her classroom. She taught me how to talk slower and breathe a certain way. This lasted several days. Mrs. Quattlebaum became my speech pathologist, a term I knew nothing about.

On Saturday, September 15, 1956, we were picking cotton for Uncle Tug and Grandma Hennie was at the house desperately ill. We picked until noon and went by Aunt Lillie's to see Grandma Hennie, but they said she was too sick to be seen. She passed that evening at 7:15 p.m. This was a sad day for our household since it was our first death to recall. Most of our other cousins stayed out of school to mourn, but Moma insisted that we go to school every day. To my recollection, I missed three days of school my whole 12 years of attending primary and secondary school.

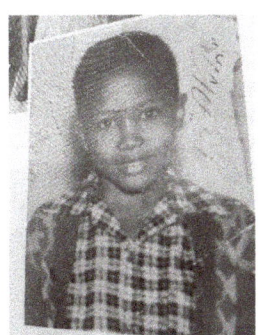

Alvin Larke - Sleepy Hollow Elementary School Picture

In fifth grade, we would have spelling competitions and lined up on each side of the classroom. I wasn't picked because of my stuttering and was often laughed at by my classmates. I was the best speller, but had not been chosen because of my inability to spell quickly due to stuttering. Mrs. Quattlebaum found favor in me. She encouraged me to forego recess and return to her classroom daily for speaking lessons, not speech pathology. I was taught to talk slower and breathe between letters. It worked. I became the top speller in my class and was invited to the District Spelling Bee at Jefferson Elementary School. I recall missing the word, SHOWER. I started the word with a "C."

One of the disappointments during my fifth grade year was an assignment to study the spelling words on page 37. When I opened my spelling book to study that night, there was no page 37. The page had been torn out. It was a used book and handed down to us from the white school. This was during the time that public education was segregated. During those times we received all used textbooks and busses simply because we were Black or Colored. The word Colored was used to describe Black people. When I reflect, this treatment was very painful when I think about how we were treated, just because we were Black. Now, I look back and see just how far we have come as Black people.

In Mr. Thomas' class. He was the only male on the faculty and very firm. He insisted that the boys were to have their shirts tucked in and were to wear belts daily. The girls had to wear ribbons in their hair daily. We enjoyed him and accepted his firm, yet meaningful method of teaching. During my sixth-grade year I was selected as the May King and Joyce Ann McDaniel was May Queen. We were honored during the Annual May Day Celebration. I graduated with excellent grades and enrolled at Jefferson High School the following fall.

During the summers, we started picking cotton the Monday after the second Sunday in August. We would pick cotton for Mr. Eldred Andrews, Uncle Jule, Uncle Albert, Uncle Tug, Rev. Bryant, Mr. Pete and ourselves, which was Daddy's field. Moma often sent each of us to different ones, so we could assist everyone with gathering their cotton.

O JEFFERSON, OUR SCHOOL SO DEAR...

The fall of 1958, I entered Jefferson High School. That morning before the school year started, after a sleepless night, I stepped on a rusty nail. My mom tied a piece of fat back and a penny. Fat back was the skin of the hog that when fried was used for seasoning vegetables. Fat back (according to Moma) would draw the poison out of my foot. I was in 7-1, the top section of the seventh grade, and spent all day hopping around between classes. My homeroom teacher was Mrs. Roberson, who taught me English. I did very well academically that year, however, I received my first C and got a whipping from my mom. I didn't receive another C while in high school. At this time, I did not get a whipping.

I remember one particular day in seventh grade very well. It was the day I was given my sisters' lunch money but the same day I decided to cut class. My sisters were unable to eat that day because I had their lunch money. I tried to make up to my sisters prior to getting home. That did not work. When they got home that afternoon, they told my mom that they were hungry because I did not give them their lunch money. My mom's whippings didn't hurt as bad as her words. Telling me that I was not responsible hurt me to the core.

Each of us had chores. Shirley and Emma washed the dishes and cleaned the house. Charles and I took care of the chickens, cows, and hogs. We also chopped wood and brought it in for cooking and heating. We had one cow at first and that cow belonged to me. Her name was Bossie, she had her first calf. Her first calf was named Scamp. Daddy sold Scamp and Bossie was milked daily, both morning and evening. I inherited milking the cow because one Saturday, after my parents returned from shopping in Augusta (town), I had milked Bossie. Moma congratulated me on how well I had done. She told me it would be my job to milk from henceforth. It later included another cow, Charles' cow, named Elsie.

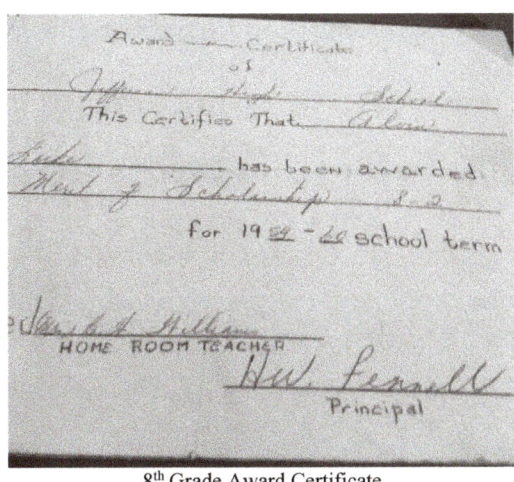

8th Grade Award Certificate

In the eighth grade, I was in Mrs. Williams' homeroom. She taught me mathematics. She validated me academically by giving me an award entitled Merit of Scholarship. It was a good year and I was inducted into the National Honor Society. I also had my first fight in eighth grade. I got on the bus early after school and sat next to Cookie. She was Bennie's girlfriend and he wanted to sit next to her. Instead, I slid over and that upset him. We argued briefly and ended up fighting. Charles and I double-teamed him. We were suspended from riding the bus but were allowed to attend school. All three of us rode with Mr. Allen, Bennie's grandfather. He dropped us off at the house of my eighth grade science teacher, Miss Green. We rode in her truck with her and her father, who dropped us off at Jefferson. On Wednesday, March 30th, we had an accident. The truck turned over in the storm. I was left in while the others were thrown out. Charles cried out that I was still in there. I heard him but couldn't say anything. I felt the acid from the battery spilling out on my gray jeans. They rescued me and I was taken to University Hospital in Augusta, GA. I had three fractured ribs on the left side. I couldn't cry nor sneeze. I was in so much pain. I was out of school for the rest of the week.

In ninth grade I met the most encouraging teacher in my life. Mr. Boston Johnson, II. He was my homeroom teacher and taught me vocational agriculture. I was initiated into the New Farmers of America. We learned the NFA Creed, something I can still recite from memory:

"I believe in the dignity of farm work and that I shall prosper in proportion as I learn to put knowledge and skill into the occupations of farming.

I believe that the farm boy who learns to produce better crops and better livestock, who learns to improve and beautify his home surroundings will find joy and success in meeting the challenging situations as they arise in his daily living.

I believe that rural organizations should develop their leaders from within; that the boys in the rural communities should look forward to positions of leadership in the civic, social and public life surrounding them.

I believe that the life of service is the life that counts; that happiness endures to mankind when it comes from having helped lift the burdens of others.

I believe in the practice of cooperation in agriculture; that it will aid in bringing to the man lowest down a wealth of giving as well as receiving.

I believe that each farm boy bears the responsibility for finding and developing his talents to the life of his people may thereby be enriched so that happiness so thar happiness and contentment will come to all."

Mr. Johnson encouraged me and insisted that I write on the chalkboard because of my excellent penmanship. He stressed my goodness and asked me not to follow the "knuckle heads." Because I wanted to take agriculture, I would have to forego two of my college preparatory courses, French II and Chemistry. Agriculture was two periods for the first two years. I took English I, Science, Algebra I, Physical Education, and Vocational Agriculture.

In my tenth grade year, I took English II, Biology, World History, Algebra II, Physical Education and Vocational Agriculture. I continued with the agriculture contest and this enhanced my leadership ability. I became secretary of my local chapter and continued in that position until I graduated from High School. One remembrance of my sophomore year was in October when the

World Series was being played. Charles refused to go to the cotton field when we got home, he wanted to watch the Yankees play the Reds. We fought because he didn't want to do as we were told. He assured me that he would play sick the next day to watch the game. The next morning, as we took the cows out, Charles fell as he staked his cow out and I returned home. Moma asked where he was and I told her. She sent me back for him but I only helped him get home. Later that morning he had an emergency appendectomy in the Aiken Hospital. Untruths will cost you and it cost Charles that day.

In eleventh grade, I enrolled in English III, Geometry, United States History, and Vocational Agriculture. I was elected as the State NFA Secretary at South Carolina State College. Mr. Johnson was very proud. My prom date during my Junior Year was Mary Ella Brown from Schofield High School. Mrs. Ashe was responsible for that happening. She asked if I had a date. I told her that I did not. Mrs. Ashe was my English teacher and my homeroom teacher in the 11th grade. Mrs. Ashe also taught me how to dance.

My 12th grade homeroom teacher was Mr. Adams. My 12th grade year was by far my most rewarding. I joined the Dukes Organization, the Dramatics Club, and I also served on the Annual

Staff. My courses that year consisted of English IV, French I, Physics, Vocational Agriculture, and Family Living.

On November 22nd, 1963, as we were sitting in our Family Living class, the announcement came over the intercom system that President John F. Kennedy had been assassinated in Dallas, Texas. That was a very morbid day and weekend at our house. To observe the television coverage was very emotional. My mom cried! It was unbelievable! The President who offered the Negroes so much has been killed and our dreams were shattered. Our pending Civil Rights Bill giving us equal rights would not happen now, we thought.

Our senior class was the first class to take a senior class trip. We visited Washington, D.C. We visited the grave of the late president John F. Kennedy. It was sad to see the eternal flame and knowing our dreams rested there. We also visited the office of the late Strom Thurmond. It was hurtful visiting Thurmond's office. He was arrogant. He told us that the Civil Rights Bill would not pass. American wasn't ready for "that" yet. We talked much about this as we left his office.

Internally, I was so frustrated. For many years, I have tried to please my dad. I even considered whether to go to college to see if it would change anything. Hindsight, I was too much like a moma's boy. My dad resented me for my ambitions and that hurt me for many years.

Our senior prom was held on April 29, 1964. My prom guest was Jo Ann Harrison from Aiken, SC.

Alvin Larke Yearbook Picture 1964

Our Commencement was held on Tuesday evening, June 2nd. I was surprised to receive the Omega Psi Phi Fraternity scholarship. Mr. Johnson is a member of that fraternity.

HAIL, HAIL DEAR SCSC...

On Sunday, September 6, 1964, it was time to depart for college. Mr. Johnson had gotten me admitted and told me, "Make something out of yourself."

My daddy said, "Boys don't go to college. They go to work or the military."

I had worked six days a week all summer at Lansdell's Florist on #1 Broad Street in Augusta, Georgia. I was paid thirty dollars a week. That was five dollars per day and I realized that working was not what I had wanted to do. I had inherited that job from my cousin, Alton, who was old enough to get a public job. I wasn't of age. Mr. Johnson called many times during the summer to find out if I had received my acceptance and whether I would be going. I made up my mind during my alone time that summer to break the curse, venture out, and attend college. I was the first from the Kathwood Community to attend college. This was indeed worth trying, and I dealt with a lot of negativity and pressure.

On the morning of my departure for college with my trunk packed, daddy told me if I wanted to go, I had to change the oil in the family vehicle, a 1958 Chevrolet, Delray. In response to all his cursing, unknowingly, I let the transmission fluid out. Daddy saw it and dragged me from under the car and said that I intended to do it. He whipped me pretty bad that Sunday morning, hoping I would not want to go to college. In getting my whipping, I decided to talk back, and remember saying, "Make it good, this is the last one!"

Moma came out and chastised me for talking back, but I had to say it. I was tossed between whether it was worth doing all of this, just to attend college.

I remember sitting in the back seat holding my younger sister, Trelle's, hand as my daddy constantly said, "You will never amount to anything."

I watched cotton fields, and said, "Goodbye." I struggle not to say anything because my mom had told me not to say anything.

We arrived on the campus and I had a room assignment in the upperclassmen dormitory, Bethea Hall. Just before leaving my mom assured me that she would support me financially and my dad made a snide remark, which I prefer not to repeat. I hugged my little sister and my mom and took two trips to get my things upstairs. I was assigned to Room 315. My roommate was Franklin Perry from Covington, Georgia. We talked awhile that night but I was getting homesick and kept reliving my day about my whipping from my dad and his remarks that I wouldn't amount to anything for my behavior.

SC State College Freshman Class 1964

We had freshman orientation all week and were assigned our classes. I was given a total of sixteen credit hours and attended classes every day, Monday through Saturday. I met many friends and still remain in contact with many of them today. I attended church every Sunday, though I said I wouldn't. We attended three churches, Trinity United Methodist Church, New Mount Zion Baptist Church, and Williams Chapel AME Church. We had Vesper Service every Sunday evening, Chapel every Friday, and had assigned seats.

My first semester didn't go well. My roommate and I didn't get along because he played clarinet and would practice at 2 a.m. without fail. That was so disturbing and caused me to be sleepy in my classes. In my history class, the professor asked me stay after class and told me that young men didn't sit on the front row. I lost all interest and sat on the back row while writing love letters the rest of the semester. I ended up getting a "D" in the course.

I received my grades during Christmas break, right after Christmas. There was a message that read, "Limited Load." In other words, Scholastic Probation. I heard "his" voice again, saying, "You will never amount to anything."

I returned to State after Christmas and prayed about my fate. I prayed daily that I could prove my dad wrong. It was my motivation to accomplish my immediate goal. That semester I received one "D" in Botany. I was off scholastic probation.

That summer I was old enough to get a regular job and worked alongside my sister Emma at Seminole Mills as a yarn supplier. The work was easy. I was praying daily about how to better myself in college, so I could make my mom proud of me, and of course Mr. Johnson.

1964 NFA Jacket

I returned to State that fall and took eighteen hours of coursework. I performed well. This time I received one "D" in Zoology. I earned B's in the other classes. *Wow, I can do this*! At least it was a thought, and I seem to be getting the hang of it. I roomed with Clyde Hightower. He was also in the School of Agriculture. We roomed in Bethea Hall, Room 327. I interviewed for a work study job in the Agriculture and Home Economics Library. Mrs. Sheffield was the Agriculture and Home Economics librarian. Mrs. Sheffield found favor in me. I worked 15 hours per week but was encouraged to study when I wasn't working with other students regarding their needs. I worked on Monday and Wednesday evenings from 7-9 p.m. and Saturday from 8 to 12noon and in between classes in Staley Building in the library. I enjoyed my work in the library and worked in that position until the spring of 1968 when I was assigned to student teach.

NFA Badge

In October, we boarded a Greyhound bus to Atlanta for the New Farmers of America (NFA) and Future Farmers of America (FFA) merging meeting. We lodged at the YMCA. It was very emotional. To see so many grown-ups sobbing made me wonder why? So much was changing with integration. The thought of it was a rough time. Our return trip was silent as we retired our Black and Gold corduroy jackets. No more NFA—had to re-learn the emblem and creed. It was so different. We received our first National FFA officer in 1984. My grades were good, but I received a "D" in Botany.

The spring semester went well though I received another "D." This time in Economics. I had to keep doing good and still strive to refute my dad's statement. I finished my sophomore year and went back to work at Seminole Mills. I worked the third shift and assisted on the family farm after I rested.

I returned to State College in the fall and was assigned to Room 226. My roommate was Junior "DA" Wade from my high school, Jefferson. I received good grades that semester. This was a better semester because I was enrolled in many of my agriculture courses. I spent the Thanksgiving holidays with my good friend, Lonnie Davis. We took the train to Florence, SC. I saw a young lady at Cumberland United Methodist Church on Sunday, November 27th, 1966. She had two little girls with her and was wearing a blue two-piece suit and a black hat. When we returned to Lonnie's house, we were sitting in the living room and I asked him who this young girl was. She was so petite and attractive. He yelled in the kitchen and asked his mom and sister. My heart sunk as they said, "You are talking about the little James girl. She is in the seventh or eighth grade." Me, being a junior in college made me question how could I be attracted to a girl so much younger.

I said never mind. That night riding back on the train, each time I closed my eyes, I saw her and prayed that she wasn't too young and that I would see her again. I know prayer works. I prepared for my final exams and did fair. No more "D's" for me. The semester ended and I had better grades.

I returned the spring semester. On Friday, January 13, 1967, I was in my room and Lonnie came down and asked me about going to a basketball game with him. His high school basketball team (Wilson) was playing Wilkerson, and he wanted me to walk with him to the game. I initially said no, but when he returned a couple minutes later, I agreed. However, we argued all the way there, because I said, "It's Friday the 13th, this is a bad luck day." People always talked about the 13th on a Friday is bad luck. It was good luck for me because I met my wife on Friday, the 13th. We also missed the girl's game.

As we sat in the bleachers, this seventh or eighth grader appears with the girls coming out of the locker room. In excitement, I yelled, "Look, Room (that's what I had called him for years), there's the girl." He was into the game. I got her attention and asked her did she want a seat." She agreed. We made little conversation, and I asked, "Do you have a boyfriend?"

She said, "Yes!"

I responded, "Girl, I am going to marry you!"

Her response, "Boy, you are a fool."

I remain with Pat until this day, "I am still a fool." That relationship has had its stormy days, but we have survived. It survived for over fifty-four years.

The semester ended and I had to attend summer school because of my grades the first semester. Again, I performed well. I took Chemistry 104 and Health Education. My roommate was my freshman roommate, Perry. I had introduced him to my first "girlfriend", Shirley. They had a strong bond and I modeled their relationship. They had a strong bond. I enjoyed seeing how they got along. I thought they were made for each other. I wanted to model their relationship.

My senior year was one of much unrest on the campus as it was nation-wide on college campuses. Segregation was real and a top issue in Orangeburg as it was in many places around the country. The first semester, we marched and protested about the inequalities downtown. We marched to integrate the Bowling Alley downtown. My Moma heard about the protest and marches and called me. She told me not to forget why I was in college and that was to get an education. She was very concerned about me as always. I listened to

Moma and finished the first semester of my senior year with good grades with all agricultural education courses. I returned the second semester to campus and was assigned to student teach at Geer Gantt High School in Belton, SC. Jay Cummings was my student teaching partner. We roomed with Mrs. Jenkins. We both performed well and returned to campus the weekend of February 3rd to take The National Teachers Examination (NTE).

There was much unrest on the campus which led to the Orangeburg Massacre that occurred on the front of the campus on Thursday, February 8th, 1968. Three young men lost their lives that bloody night. Their names were Henry Smith, Samuel Hamilton and Delano Middleton. Many others were injured. This was a very sad occasion for all students on the campuses of South Carolina State College, Claflin University and Wilkinson Senior High School, the local high school. Smith, Hamilton and Middleton were shot in the back, running from the police. The campus gymnasium is named after them.

We completed our student teaching on Friday, March 12th, and received excellent evaluations from our student teacher supervisor, Mr. Harold J. Mackey. We returned to campus, and I was sought out to be the first of my class to receive an interview. I was scheduled to interview on April 5, 1968 for a teaching position in St. Matthews, Calhoun County. The evening before, Dr. Martin Luther King, Jr. was assassinated. A group of us were playing "spades" when the news came across the television that Dr. King had been shot. I feared going to my interview because of the unrest surrounding that the death of Dr. King. Feelings of what the future held for Blacks and how I would persevere during my interviews. I asked Robert Livingston to borrow his 1967 Chevrolet Super Sport to drive to the interview in St. Matthews. After a very sleepless night, I wondered should I cancel the interview. I thought about my dad's saying you will never amount to anything. The words provided the fuel for me to go on the interview. I was awakened with hope that I should go and perform the best I knew how.

I interviewed with the principal and superintendent. The interview went well. At least, I thought so! My grade on the NTE was not mentioned. I received an offer and accepted the second week in May.

I purchased my first car on Monday, May 20, 1968, a Grecian Green Chevelle, Super Sport 396. My mom supported me financially.

I graduated from SC State College on Sunday afternoon, May 26, 1968.

CALHOUN COUNTY, JOHN FORD HIGH SCHOOL

I arrived in St. Matthews on Sunday, June 30, 1968, after working at the Riverside Mills in Augusta, Georgia with my dad for the five weeks following my graduation from State. I arrived at the principal's home. He took me to the home of Mrs. Whaley and she wasn't at home. Then he took me to Mrs. Hattie Hopkins' home. I boarded with her. I paid her forty dollars per month, and she prepared two meals for me daily. Breakfast and supper.

John Ford High School was the Black high school in the town of St. Matthews. It was located on Agnes Street which was half a block from where I lived on Upper Muller Street.

I started work on, Monday, July 1st. It was a great first day. I was given the key to my classroom and begin readying my room to suit my taste. I prepared the bulletin board and all the little details, arranging my desk as Mr. Johnson had done at Jefferson. The principal, Mr. Parker, took to me to meet several prominent farmers in the community, the first being Mr. Nathaniel Heatley. He and I remained like father and son until his death on April 20, 1998. He had requested that I deliver his eulogy upon his passing. I flew to

South Carolina from Texas to deliver his eulogy. I taught several of the Heatleys, including the first female, in agriculture. Mr. and Mrs. Heatley were raising three of their grandsons at the time that I taught as well.

That week, I met many of my students and the parents: The Heatleys, Joneses, Kellers, Murphs, Wannamakers, Williamses, and Zieglers, just to name a few! I also met the Home Economics teacher, Mrs. Ossa B. Paris. We worked in the Community Cannery during the summer. Local families would bring their vegetables to the cannery. Mrs. Paris and I would assist them with sorting, washing, blanching, and canning.

On Friday, August 9th, I drove home because Pat was taking the bus back from Florida and was stopping in Augusta. I met her, proposed and placed a ring on her finger. I had asked her parents long before for her hand in marriage. Her dad didn't say much, but her mother was very vocal and against it! She said I had my degrees and Pat needed to get hers. She told me that once we were married, she would no longer support Pat in her education. We were determined not to let that hamper our desire to get married. So I drove Pat to Florence that Sunday afternoon, very happy. But, I was totally surprised by Mrs. James' remarks, instead of being supportive, she was disappointed. We went by my Aunt Florence's house and told her. She was excited for us. We originally set our wedding date for December 21, 1968. I found out that my "twin first cousin," Albert Larke, Jr., had set his wedding for that day. I would be his best man and he would be mine since we planned that many years prior. He was marrying the girl he dated in high school, Vera Butler. Pat and I instead planned our wedding for April 5, 1969.

Pat applied to Paine College in Augusta, GA. I drove over to pick Pat up on Friday afternoon. She and I traveled back to Augusta. I was in Alma Jones and Lawrence Dunbar's wedding that Saturday. Pat moved into the dormitory that Sunday afternoon. She and my cousin, Georgia, were roommates who was also a bridesmaid in our wedding. They have remained best friends since that time.

Mrs. Hopkins' kids were teachers, so she had a lot of motherly advice for me. She said, "Alvin, don't smile the first semester."

I said, "Mrs. Hopkins, I have always been a smiling person."

She said, "Your smiling face will allow the children to take advantage of you."

I thanked her and went my merry way. Needless to say, I smiled, yet I was very firm with my students.

The paddle could be used during that time and I used it. Most of the students were really 'trying' me. My first major encounter came after I had been on the job just six weeks. I asked a student to be quiet and after several times asking him, he replied, "Make me!"

The other students laughed and I became frustrated. I headed toward the student and was relieved when I got to his desk. I had silently prayed that he would leave prior to me getting to his desk. When I got there, the student was gone. I know what prayer can do! That wasn't the end of the story! The principal returned with the student and said, "He will stay in here if you don't."

I was already ticked off, so I gathered my belongings and left the school. I sped off in my 1968 SS and drove home. I told my Moma what happened, and she listened as she was preparing supper. After our meal, my Moma told me, "Alvin, you can't let children run you away."

As I drove back to St. Matthews that night, I thought about what I would say to the student. I asked him not to return to my class and he didn't. He returned to my class the next year. I am glad that I listened to my Moma.

My students performed well in all Future Farmer of America (FFA) contests. It was my goal to win a state contest and become the president of the State Association. My chapter won several district contests. We climbed the ladder and were successful. John Ford FFA was on the maps, purchasing jackets, entering all contests, and doing great things in the community.

The faculty were very receptive of the FFA group and the changes that I had brought to the agriculture department. The community embraced me and the students.

Alvin and Pat Larke married April 5, 1969

April came quickly. Pat and I were married on April 5, 1969, at Cumberland United Methodist Church, Florence. This was the same church where I had first seen her in November of 1966.

We had an argument on that Friday before our wedding. We didn't speak because Pat was supposed to be in St. Matthews at noon, but showed up at four that afternoon with the excuse that they had car problems. My brother Johnnie and cousins (Georgia and Ella) were together. My tenth grade student and close friend Charles Jones and I had been waiting. It seemed like forever.

The officiating minister asked, "What wrong with you all?"

Neither of us responded. I felt terrible all night and called the next morning to ask whether she was going to show up for our wedding. The wedding was scheduled at 11 a.m. on the Saturday before Easter. Her bridal party never responded. They stayed at Pat's paternal grandma's house and the groom's party stayed at the Davis' residence.

When I saw my bride on the arm of her father approaching the altar, I forgot about yesterday and the night before. We spent our honeymoon in Rocky Mount, North Carolina. We arrived late that evening after a reception at the church. We stayed there until Monday and Pat went back to my parent's. She had to move off campus because she was married. I returned to St. Matthews.

I finished the school year and began being plagued by the Selective Service about being drafted. Having the status of a teacher was supposed to assist with my deferment, but it didn't have any impact. So I continued teaching, because of the Viet Nam War, I was needed. I worked throughout the summer because I had a twelve month contract. I was visiting students with their animal projects, the cannery, FFA Leadership Camp, and Summer Camp. I was allowed two weeks of summer vacation. Pat and I moved into our first home, 110 Upper Muller Street, St. Matthews. This house was rented to us by the high school principal and his wife, the Parkers.

On the first Monday in September, Pat experienced early morning sickness. We went to several doctors because she couldn't be pregnant. She was on the pill. Finally, a doctor in Cameron confirmed that she was indeed pregnant and would have the baby April 16, 1970. It was bittersweet, and we were very quiet because her mother had said that I had my degree and would leave her with a house full of children, and she would never get a college degree like I did. We didn't talk for a few days, which seemed like weeks. People were told to start counting. Mrs. James said: "I told you so. It was so important for Pat to finish her education. Pat gained employment at the bank in Columbia, carrying a bucket to work every morning because of morning sickness. It was so traumatic! We were not happy having a child so early. Now all of Pat's educational endeavors were put on hold. Our planned protection efforts did not work. The doctor indicated that nothing is 100% other than abstinence.

During the fall semester, I received my official letter. I was being drafted. I immediately went to the local National Guard Unit. They had NO Blacks in the Unit. The Viet Nam War was going on and I was needed. This was another huddle, but for that, much happens for that town. Many Blacks joined this SC National Guard after the race barrier was broken.

That was a NO NO. But God in His infinite wisdom allowed the SC National Guard Unit to permit the admittance of three Blacks, James "Pete" Amaker, Thomas Carson, and Alvin Larke, Jr., to enter. We had many obstacles but continued to bond together. Pete and I have continued to remained close friends.

We had to do six months of active duty, return to our unit for one weekend per month, and two weeks of annual training per year. I reported to duty in late January to Fort Bragg for Basic Combat

Training (BCT). I was told many times that I was in the wrong line. I was supposed to be drafted (US), or volunteered (RA), but not a National Guardsman (NG). I had developed an upper respiratory infection and was placed in the infirmary. I was told that unless I was out by a certain day, I would have to be recycled. Recycle means, I would have to start Basic Training over from the beginning. This would delay my returning home time for four weeks. I outsmarted the system. I placed ice in my mouth prior to my temperature being taken and was discharged that afternoon. I graduated from BCT the latter part of March and was assigned to Fort Eustis, Virginia, for Advanced Individual Training (AIT). My Military Occupational Specialist (MOS) was Helicopter Crew Chief (67N20). In training, I performed well and was often told that I would perform those duties in Vietnam. I didn't say anything, because I knew I would be returning home at the end of my training.

April 16th came and went, and no baby had been born. I called collect several days inquiring as to how Pat was doing. She was very depressed. That bothered me because I blamed myself. When I arrived back to the barracks on Monday, May 4th, after class, I was told that I was the father of an infant daughter. She was born at 11:38

a.m. that morning and weighed six pounds. I drove home that weekend and held my daughter for the first time. I looked at her most of the night. She was named Altricia Wilretha which is a combination of our first names and our mothers' first names.

I returned home on June 17th after completing my training at Fort Eustis, VA. I started back to work at John Ford. I worked during my regular summer schedule. This was really working in our favor because it was supplemental income. I spent time with Pat and Altricia being the husband and father I always aspired to become.

CALHOUN COUNTY PART 2: 1970-1980

It was great getting back to my students. They were glad I was back. Pat took a position as a teacher's aide at Bethlehem Elementary School. She was assigned to Mrs. Donnell S. Keitt. This was really working in our favor. It was supplemental income. We continued to do well and joined Bethel AME Church. Our daughter was baptized. Joan and Lonnie Davis became her godparents along with Pauline H. Jones. Lonnie Davis was my college roommate and Joan was Lonnie's sister. We had been long time friends and they attended Pat's home church, Cumberland. Pauline Jones was Mr. Heatley's daughter. Both of them were very supportive of us. Remember Lonnie was responsible for our meeting. He insisted that I attend the basketball game that night, Friday, the 13th.

Our daughter became the community baby with many babysitters. She was often taken for rides with students and loved by my students, especially the Larrymore family. They lived down the street and were easily accessible. Tricia (as we called her) and I usually took day trips while Pat worked at the local Winn Dixie on Saturdays. We would visit Pat's parents, grandparents, or my parents, and be back home by the time Pat got off from work. After working as a teacher's aide for one year, Pat decided to go back to school. She enrolled at SC State and declared Elementary Education as her major. She did very well academically. She made the honor roll every semester and continued to work at the Winn Dixie.

After a brief encounter with a student, I decided to return to South Carolina State and pursue my master's degree. I pride myself with excellent penmanship. It had been documented from my elementary school days and throughout high school. This particular day after copying a test and administering it to my student, he didn't perform well. I asked, "Why?"

He responded that he couldn't read my writing. When given the test orally, he responded well and scored a high "B." I decided then to get my Master's in Special Education. I performed well and was in a class with my eighth grade science teacher, Ms. Josephine Green.

We were ordered to desegregate that year. The campus I worked at would only be ninth and tenth grades. St. Matthews High would be eleventh and twelfth graders. Our principal made a big deal out of it and had us preparing for the "white" students. The teachers made preparation for the students. It was a critical time, but I have to admit it made me a bit nervous. Finding that all students were alike and learned at a level of different just as Black students.

FFA Students circa 1979

I found out when they arrived that there were the same kind of students of both ethnicities. I involved all of my students in the FFA and had one white student participate. His mother would not allow him to travel with the team, but she would pick him up after school. It hurt me to leave him at school standing outside of the fence waiting to be picked up. He decided against his mother's wishes. I was allowed to drop him off near the home but was not allowed in his yard. Rather sad, but I supported him, and he was able be a significant team member to our Soil Judging Team.

Pat and I were both in school at the same time. She was an honor student in her undergraduate studies. I took courses in the evenings and Saturdays. My maternal grandmother died on May 8, 1972. We had stopped by her house that Sunday, April 30th, and she died that Monday. It was the first death that impacted our lives since our paternal grandmother in 1956. My last conversation with her was the Sunday, April 30th, night before her death. She was jovial and in good spirits. I had passed her house and Pat said: "Larke, you ought to stop and just say "hi". I just turned around and visited her. My Grandmother always shared jokes and fun times. That night she chased me around the car playing "tag." I jumped in the car and closed the door. When I let the window down she tagged me. I remembered that night with great memories as I watched her run to the porch. Pat and I talked as I drove to St. Matthews. Pat remarked of how happy we made "Mother." As we drove back home that night, we discussed Mother's behavior and the impact she had on our lives. Not knowing this was our last time to see her alive. Mother's funeral was held on Mother's Day,

In February of 1973, Pat found out that she was pregnant with our second child. She made it very clear that she was not going to have another baby in a one-bedroom house. We were disappointed because this was totally an unexpected pregnancy. We began

51

looking for houses and found one in Orangeburg. It was financed through the Farmer's Home Administration (FHA).

It happened when we were out of school for the blizzard that occurred in February. We prepared to move and did in May of 1973. Our address was Route 4, Box 120U, Orangeburg, SC 29115. Pat completed her junior year at State. That summer we landscaped our home and fenced in the backyard and property. We were very happy with our decision to move to Orangeburg. Altricia was accepted at Felton Laboratory School on State College campus at the age of three-and-a-half. She was told to be very obedient to her teachers. In September, her teacher told her to get off the merry-go-round, and she did just that! The merry-go-round was in full speed and she jumped off and broke her leg. She was on crutches for about two months.

The baby was due on October 10th. Pat was still attending classes and refused to drop out! She was determined to graduate in May of 1974. Aaron was born on Monday morning, October 15, 1973, at 3:46 a.m. He weighed 6 pounds, 10 ounces. As I sat in the waiting room, the nurse came in and said, "Clarke, a baby boy."

I told her my name was Larke.

She said, "You are the only one in here!"

I went in and took a look at the little fella, and said, "Yes, he is mine!" I went back home, got Altricia ready for school, and went to school excited that Aaron had arrived. Both of our children were named before birth, though we didn't know their gender. Aaron was my mother's maiden name, and she hadn't given any of us that name. I visited Aaron every day in the hospital. He had jaundice that required him to stay in the hospital. I visited him daily and talked to him as if he understood. Our house felt different with a room set up as nursery and no baby.

Pat was strong and reassuring that Aaron would be fine and she was right -- he was. Pat came home on Wednesday and he came home on Saturday. Tricia was excited to have her baby brother home. Altricia and Aaron have been a joy to their father even while enduring ups and downs. We had our pigeon pair, a girl and a boy. They became very close and have remained close through their lives.

The nurse told me, "You know he doesn't know you are here."

I responded, "I know I am here!"

Pat went back to classes after two weeks. Mrs. Jackson, a neighbor, came in and kept Aaron until Pat returned from classes daily.

Pat student taught in the spring of 1974. She performed well and I begin taking Aaron to St. Matthews with me in the mornings. Mrs. Floyd kept him along with two other children. She lived near the school, so it was very convenient for me to take him there in the mornings and pick him up him in the afternoons.

I continued to be a vital part of my students' lives. A positive male figure for many of them, with or without a father in the home. I had begun to love impacting the lives of young men. Only boys were allowed to take agriculture at the time. My students were actively involved in all of the FFA contests. Each summer we would attend State FFA Contest, FFA Leadership, and FFA Summer Camp.

Being like Boston Johnson became more and more a part of me as I encouraged kids to attend college and make something of themselves. They didn't have to study agriculture, just seek higher education or become gainfully employed.

After John Ford became a junior high school, I was teaching pre-vocational (shop) classes since there were no Agriculture III students at the school any longer. I was impacting more students now and giving more hands-on experience. The shop students were not required to join the FFA but the agriculture students were required.

Our family continued to strive and became active at Bethel AME Church, St. Matthews. Both of our children were baptized there. Aaron's godparents were named as Donnell and Joseph Keitt and Jacob Heatley. I was active on the Steward Board, Sunday School, Male Ensemble, Usher and advisor to the Youth Choir. Pat was active in the Women's Missionary Society and the Sunday School.

We made plans to purchase property in the rural area for me to continue my love for chickens. We purchased property from the Joneses, a one-acre plot and an additional eight acres adjacent to the one acre we had previously purchased. We started looking at plans and when the appropriate time for construction. We knew we wanted Marion Mack, a local African American builder, to build our home. Mr. Mack had built several homes in the community and we appreciated his dedication to his work.

The construction started in the spring of 1977. It was very difficult to leave Red Bank because we had many excellent neighbors. Our children were close to their school and had developed excellent friends. Our new house was huge to us. Three bedrooms, three living areas, kitchen, two dining areas, two and a half baths, laundry room, back deck, and a two-car carport.

We loved it and my dad finally said after walking through the house and over the acreage, "Son, I am very proud of you!" I had done things that my four brothers hadn't done. I had become a member of the Masonic Lodge, like Daddy and had enlisted in the military, as Daddy had. I tried to do at least two things he had done. But it was never enough.

Wow, it had taken me 31 years to gain his approval. That moment didn't last long.

I was moving up in my professional organization, South Carolina Vocational Agricultural Teacher's Association (SCVATA) and became president-elect during 1978-79 and would be elevated to the presidency in 1979-80. This allowed me to travel to the

National Vocational Agricultural Teacher's Association (NVATA) in Dallas, Texas and then in Los Angeles, California. This exposure allowed me the opportunity to be asked by two Predominantly White Institutions (PWI) to consider entering a doctoral program. I thought I had enough education and had no desire to further my education. I had my High School Principal's Certificate and was set for life, or so I thought.

Girls were allowed to take agriculture in 1978. I had five of the highly academic girls enrolled in my class, Verneta Bull, Shelia Caldwell, Angela Colter, Sharon Goodwine and Jacqueline Heatley. I had taught Jackie's older brothers and knew her family very well. That year, Sharon entered the Speaking Contest. She won the District Public Speaking Contest and went on to compete in the State Contest, which she won. A brilliant young lady. One of my professional goals was then checked off. My chapter had previously won several District FFA Contests, but not a State FFA Contest. Thanks, Sharon.

During the 1979-80 school year, St. Matthews' FFA Chapter under my leadership set the bar. My four girls won the State Soil Judging Contest and flew to Oklahoma City for the National FFA

Soil Judging Contest, a dream come true. The first group of all girls to enter and win the district and advance to the State Contest and won. During the summer of 1980, Frank Parker, our local FFA President, was elected as the State FFA President. I now felt the pride Boston Johnson felt when I was elected State NFA President in 1964. He was the first African American to be elected in the State of South Carolina. My goals and objectives as a high school agriculture teacher had been fulfilled.

It was in 1980, the same year that Pat suggested that we consider our doctorates. We decided on the University of Missouri-Columbia. We were met with much opposition from our immediate families. Pat had had a difficult year with her principal and wanted to leave the school district.

My dad said once again, "You shouldn't leave your home and a job and work toward another degree." This was another disappointment to him and others. Yet, it was a bitter/sweet decision for me. Again, I has to step out on faith. While my dad had a valid point, I wished that I did not shared so much about the University, the student population and being the second African American person enrolled in the Agricultural Education program.

We rented our two-and-a-half-year-old home out, withdrew our SC State Retirement, and moved to Missouri to pursue our doctorates. I went to school full time. Pat took a teaching position at Jefferson (Jeff) Jr. High, teaching mathematics, and went to school part time.

Leaving the St. Matthews area was painful, having lived there for 12 years. We were leaving the relationships with so many and it left us broken hearted for a while.

ON TO MISSOURI

We packed up our belongings including FiFi, our pet collie. We had packed for several weeks to include most of our clothes. We decided to rent our home to the Glovers'. We had all intentions of returning to our two-and-a-half-year-old home after completing our doctorates. The Glovers were very dear friends of ours and church members at Bethel A.M.E. Church.

We took our two cars. We drove one and towed another behind a U-Haul as we headed out for Columbia, Missouri, on Sunday afternoon, July 20, 1980. We drove straight through to Missouri. Wash Jones, Jonathan Williams, Pat, Altricia, Aaron and I, made the trip. Jonathan and I drove the UHaul and Aaron rotated from one vehicle to the other. We left our orange Ford pickup truck with Dennis Larrymore.

Wash had been with us since his first year of elementary school. I met him in the cotton field off of Highway 6 and had been mentoring him since we met. He was always our baby sitter for our children. He was Saluatorian of his high school class and had been accepted to Clemson University. Jonathan was from a family of nine children. I had known him for many years and he had taken my classes in high school. He was an excellent student.

Wash decided that he would move with us and enroll at the University of Missouri-Columbia (UMC). He majored in Agricultural Journalism. After talking to Jonathan while we traveled to Missouri, the question came up, "What if I got you accepted into UMC?"

He said he would ask his parents when he returned, but he definitely was interested. Jonathan flew back to South Carolina and his parents agreed that he could to return to UMC for schooling. I was instrumental in getting him and Wash admitted to the university because of who I was at the time. The University respected my decision and admitted Wash in Agricultural Journalism and Jonathan in Agricultural Education.

I was assigned to work in the Dean of Agriculture Office as an academic advisor. I was excited about this position. It would allow me to continue molding the lives of young scholars as I had done the past 12 years in Calhoun County.

We moved into the Nelson's four bedroom home that was fully furnished. Dr. Nelson was an Agronomy professor at the Univerisity of Missouri-Columbia who was on sabbatical for the academic year, 1980-81. A four-bedroom home, with all four bedrooms on the second floor. Our new address was Route 4, Box 210C, Columbia, MO 69501. The Route 4 felt like a connection we made a connection to our previous address: Route 4, Box 120 U, Orangeburg and Route 4, Box 237C, Orangeburg. We laughed as we talked about the connection.

I was awarded the George Washington Carver Fellowship. I had to study Agronomy as my support area and conduct research in that area.

I supervised student teachers for the Agricultural Education Department. I enrolled in twelve hours the first semester. My courses in Ag, Education and Adult Education were less challenging than Agronomy and Research and Statistics. I worked twenty hours in the Dean's office as required to fulfill the requirements for my fellowship. I got to know most of the minorities at the university and many of them transferred to the College of Agriculture under my advising. I was able to assist and mentor many student from various colleges where they were not performing well. I became popular very quickly as a "saviour" for minority and other students who found themselves in academically challenging situations. I had recruited three undergraduate and a graduate student from South Carolina. My second semester at the university, I enrolled in seventeen hours. This was allowed because I asked to complete my doctorate within two years and be degreed in August of 1982.

The summer of 1981, I enrolled in eleven hours of coursework. We flew Altricia and Aaron back to South Carolina since Pat and I were heavily engaged in our studies. We searched for a home and found one on the northside of Columbia. It was four bedrooms, three on the main floor and one in the lower part or basement. Jonathan and Wash shared a bedroom downstairs and we lived on the upper floor. We searched all summer for that house and was glad to call it home, 1108 South Victoria Avenue.

In the fall of 1981, I enrolled in 12 hours of coursework and received my first "C". Very disheartening! Another student and I had the same grades and he persuaded me to go with him to professor's office because it must have been a mistake. We had missed the same amount of classes, and had the same numerical grades on all papers, yet he received a "B", and I a "C". He saw us entering his office and yelled that he knew why we were coming and the grades were final. I contemplated filing my first discriminatory suit. My major professor said, "It's not worth it, a 'C' won't matter in the end." This was very stressful for me in many aspects.

It didn't. I completed my dissertation and defended it in time for Summer Commencement, held August 6, 1982. The title of my dissertation was, "Assessment and Evaluation of the Curriculum and Other Academic Requirements of an Undergraduate Agronomy Program in a Major Land Grant University." The findings were presented at the National Agronomy Association Meeting in Washington, DC in 1983.

The university immediately offered me an assistant professor position and I accepted. I continued to work half-time in the dean's office and half-time in the Agricultural Education department. It was a very productive academic environment because I was still able to work with students.

I begin to feel the calling to the ministry. I had become very close to the pastor at St. Paul AME Church where my family and I were very active members. During one of my annual training camps at Camp Ripley, Minnesota, I heard an audible voice, "When are you going to do as I have called you to do?" This was a fearful moment for me! I had heard this voice many times in my life, but this was an audible one. It was like He was right over my bed. I had not answered this calling since adolescence for many reasons, personal and professional. First, it involved so much time as I always knew it would. Secondly, of the "worldly things", I enjoyed playing cards and dancing.

I sat up in bed and saw no one in the barracks, but me. I responded, "When I finish my doctorate, I will accept my calling to the ministry." It was again a bittersweet moment, being fearful, I had agreed. I had given an answer, and now wondered how I would keep my word. I had done several messages from the the pulpit and been designated as a "lay speaker." But, now, this would affect my lifestyle and my family's. And Revs. Boston, Bryant, Harris or Finley had done such. They were my mentors in the ministry. Having a commitment was easy, but completing the course work and working full time at a major research institution was a bit much.

I accepted my call to the ministry on September 19, 1982, at St. Paul AME Church, Columbia, Missouri, under the leadership of Rev. Paul Harris. I enrolled in the required course work and traveled to St. Louis on weekends to fulfill all requirements. I was very successful with the coursework.

In the fall of 1983, I pledged Alpha. It was three of us and the other two decided to drop, so I dropped also. In the spring of 1984, I alone reapplied to become a member of Alpha Phi Alpha Fraternity, Inc., and was accepted as a lone candidate. I had had the desire to become a member of this fraternity since my undergraduate years at SC State.

It was during this semester that Purdue University and Texas A&M University showed an interest in me as a suitable candidate for an assistant professor position. I applied for both positions and was granted an interview by both. However, Texas A&M offered Pat and me a package deal. We interviewed there and wanted a sign. The weather was very hot and humid when we flew there, so that was a negative sign. We could barely breathe when we got off the plane in College Station.

As we checked into our room and prepared for the night, I said to Pat, "If there is an AME Church here, that's a positive sign." I wanted to complete my ministerial studies. I looked in the phone book and there it was, Allen Chapel AME Church, Bryan, Texas.

We were both was successful in our interviews, Pat in the College of Education and I in the College of Agriculture. We discussed the pros and cons of acceptance of our offers there. From the childrens' grade levels, promotions to the next rank or moving before Pat finished her doctorate were part of our decision making. We were convinced that it was in our best interest to accept the offers. Pat was offered the position as a Visiting Assistant Professor in the College of Education and I was offered the position of Assistant Professor of Agricultural Education. At this time, Pat was beginning to collect data and write her dissertation.

We took the family down to Texas in May and made the decision after returning to accept the positions. We had several conversations with Jonathan and Wash about their decisions. Wash decided to join us and move to Texas, Jonathan decided to remain in Columbia. I had recruited three other African American males, Franklin Delano Benson, Jacob Heatley, and Curtis D. White. Benson was a freshman. Jacob was a transfer student from Clemson University. Curtis was a teacher in South Carolina that entered the master's program at the University of Missouri.

I completed the requirements and was initiated into Alpha Phi Alpha Fraternity, Inc., on Friday evening, July 13, 1984. Pat and I drove to Texas on Sunday, July 15th. Pat assisted me in getting settled in and flew back to Missouri two days later.

I begin searching for a place for us to live once the family arrived in mid-August. The realtor had shown us several places while Pat was in town, but we weren't impressed with any of the properties. Pat returned to Missouri via plane, packed up, and returned with family and the family pet, FiFi, in mid-August.

TEXAS A&M UNIVERSITY AND THE COMMUNITY 1984-1990 (PART 1)

We were blessed to find a home for rent on Glade Street. It was 1402 Glade and in an excellent community. We got along with the neighbors and often walked in the community. The house had four bedrooms, three upstairs, and the master bedroom was downstairs. It was a unique setup. The backyard was fenced so that FiFi could have a place to run and play. My starting date was July 16, 1984. I lived in an efficiency until I found that place for the family.

Pat and the family arrived the early part of August with a U-Haul and we begin to unpack. We (Pat and I) were actively involved with new faculty orientation. It started on August 21, 1984 and ended that Friday. It was very informative, but challenging.

The following week, we got Altricia and Aaron registered in their schools. Altricia was at A&M Consolidated and Aaron was at Oakwood Middle School. They adjusted well! One of us dropped Altricia off and Aaron rode his bike to school.

I was given my teaching assignment and was assigned to 105B Scoates as my office. Other than teaching or assisting with student teachers, I was teaching three sections of AGED 440, Principles of

Technological Change. It met Monday, Wednesday, and Friday at 8, 9, and 10 a.m. for 50 minutes per day. The students took a liking to me, like they had done since teaching high school. There would always be one or two who would test me, but my entire time at Texas A&M University, my students continued to be my prize possessions. Overall, they were excellent.

During this time, I was considered a neophyte in the fraternity and desired to have an undergraduate chapter at TAMU. I met another fraternity member upon my arrival and we talked about the possibility of getting an undergraduate chapter on this predominantly white campus. We made an appointment with Dr. Koldus. He thought our suggestion needed to go before the president of the university. We made an appointment with Dr. Koldus, Vice President of Student Services. He thought our suggestion needed to go before the president of the university. We met with Dr. Vandiver, President, and he assured us that there would never be a fraternity on campus. The Corps of Cadets would be the closest and only fraternity organized on TAMU's campus. This was difficult for me as my colleagues had heard that I could go to the president office. They assured mne that serving as an advisor for the Colleagiate FFA was more than enough for me. My request was to afford young men the same thing I had received, mentorship. Since 1984, over 250 brothers have become Alphas because of that season of wanting academic leadership and mentoring. We continued to press the issue and contrary to what many faculty thought to be a losing battle, we found 11 young men. They were academically talented individuals interested in being initiated into Alpha Phi Alpha Fraternity. Thus, mentoring formally begin.

My office was inundated with many students, mostly minority. I advised the fraternity and the gospel choir. This was against the wishes of other faculty, as it was not considered to be related to tenure and promotion. I also advised the Collegiate Chapter of FFA. Although it went against the wishes and wants of administration, I saw a need to assist as many students as I could, especially those who were underserved.

I did most of my writing in the evening. I would go home and have supper with the family and return to campus, often walking. It was my time to reflect and thank God for His goodness to me. I was blessed to be a blessing to others. I was assigned as pastor of St. James AME Church, Calvert, Texas. My first Sunday there was

October 7, 1984. The congregation consisted of eight senior citizens, all widowed except one, and retired. The church was white-framed, no piano, and no restroom facilities. There was a lot of work to be done.

The first semester was hectic. I was also assisting Pat in completing her dissertation. I lost the document a couple of times. I used the office computer in my building to type in what she had written on a daily basis. This worked well and she was able to defend her dissertation in March, 1985. She was successful and graduated in May of that year. We traveled by car to Columbia and witnessed her receiving her doctorate in Educational Administration. Jonathan received his undergraduate degree in Agricultural Education. Upon Pat's graduation, she was given the rank of Assistant Professor in her department. Jonathan received his undergraduate degree in Agricultural Education.

Our beloved Fifi died of heartworms fall of that year. Fifi was a part of our family since 1975. She was well-trained and loved our kids. The year went by swiftly! We moved to 1222 South Ridgefield Circle after two years on Glade Street. It was an excellent move. A one story house, very accommodating, with a fenced backyard, and a drive-through garage. It was a very good neighborhood. We lived there for three years. During that time I experienced my second back surgery in the spring of 1987. It was a tough surgery, but I survived it and returned to the campus the latter part of the semester. I had survived a previous back surgery in January 1980. I never found out what caused my back surgery. My Mother said that it came from me walking at 8 months old.

Then came the long road of publishing or perishing. I would publish and not succumb to what many had doubts about. I found it hard to believe how many negative comments we heard from both Blacks and whites. Two stand out, "You can't preach and teach, it's one or the other." Another, "A&M is very racist, and you all won't be successful. Never!" Both of those individuals didn't live to see either of us reach the top. I can truly say, "But God!"

The spring semester of 1985, I started teaching graduate courses and was assigned to work with the Young Farmers of Texas. These assignments were met with great enthusiasm. Teaching graduate classes allowed me to serve on graduate student committees and eventually chair my first graduate student committee. This also assisted me with co-authoring journal articles that helped with receiving tenure and promotion.

On December 18, 1988, we saw a home for lease in the College Station area. It would allow me to have chickens, which I hadn't had since I left South Carolina in 1980. We looked at the home prior to leaving for South Carolina for Christmas. We were under a lease at the home on Ridgefield and wondered how we could break the lease. The person leasing said we would have to pay the agreed amount until the lease expired in June of that year. We couldn't afford that, but Dr. Bertrand, a professor in the Engineering Department, owned the home and allowed us to move in paying nothing until our lease ceased on Ridgefield.

We moved there and were content for the years we lived there.

In the fall of 1987, I, being an itinerant elder in the AME Church, was called into the Office of Bishop Stokes in Houston, Texas. He told me that he was moving me from Calvert and Hearne to become pastor of St. John in Brenham. I objected, and was asked whether I was Methodist or Baptist.

I responded. "Methodist."

He responded, "I am sending you."

I told Pat and we cried that night at our hotel as we had increased St. James from eight members to thirty-five. We had purchased a piano for the church and built two restrooms. It was difficult to leave that congregation. However, we left and were well received at St. John in Brenham. That congregation grew and entertained several annual conferences during our tenure there.

Everything at A&M continued to remain positive and my first six years swiftly passed. In the fall of 1989, I was called in by my department head, who told me that I was being considered for promotion to Associate Professor with tenure. I asked for guidelines and was told that there were none. This was very difficult because others has received tenure and promotion after six years of service. I, being the only Black, had to submit a packet with no instructions. I felt frustrated in putting together a tenure packet of my work. I was the first one in my department to develop a packet. Having no guidelines to follow, I spent much time gathering information for my packet. I was afraid of not having done enough and about advising groups outside of the department. Much advice from others but also support.

I submitted my packet during the fall of 1989, and was given approval at the department, college and university level without any negative remarks. At their March meeting, in 1990, the Board of Regents voted unanimously and I was granted promotion to the rank of Associate Professor with tenure at Texas A&M University. I was very proud of the honor and was excited for the next step in the process.

PART 2

In the fall semester of 1990, I was challenged to create a new curriculum; instead of General Agriculture, Agriculture Development. I chaired a committee, consisting of several faculty members in the department. This degree appealed to many students from other majors and increased the diversity in our department. I enjoyed the work and most of all, the success of the students, along with the growth of the student population in the department.

Our daughter decided that Texas A&M University wasn't a good fit for her. She was a brilliant student but had not done well. She wanted to go to South Carolina State University and with much apprehension, we agreed. She was a Biology/Pre-Med Student. She matriculated well, but in the spring of 1991, she became pregnant and Pat went to South Carolina to get her and she returned home. This was one of the worse years of my life. Altricia being pregnant and Aaron running away from home. I nor Pat deserve this, but it happened.

Aaron ran away his senior year of high school and was doing very well academically. During the week that he was supposed to be on his senior class trip, I was told that he was seen in town. When he returned home, he said he had gone on the trip. He became combative and ran away from home. He didn't return and moved in with some college students. He didn't finish high school and later received his GED. That was the beginning of him traveling down the wrong road. As an Assoicate Professor at a major university, the pastor of number one Church in the Brenham district, how was I to face the congregation on Sunday or my classes at A&M? How could I effectively lead a congregation or effectively teach and advise students when my own home was in disarray? It was simple, hindsight, trust the Maker and Creator of every good and perfect gift, God. I was very concerned about the perception of others at the time.

In the spring of 1991, I was awarded a plaque, watch, and monetary award for being an Outstanding Teacher at the University. This was due to student evaluations and faculty support. Very prestigious!

In March of that year after being asked to be the speaker at Somerville ISD's Black History program, I met my last "son." He introduced me as their guest speaker and he became another mentee. His teachers and guidance counselor counted him out. They said he was not good enough to enter or matriculate at Texas A&M. I begged to differ. I merely wanted them to see with proper mentoring what one could and would do. I had him admitted as one of the four Jumpstart students. At Texas A&M I created a program for non-traditional students entitled, "Ag Jumpstart." This program allowed me to select him as a student. As a part of the program, students attended summer classes, making a grade point of 3.0 or better, then enrolling in the fall as a student.

He received three degrees in nine years and was one of the youngest to have received so many degrees in such a short span. He had a horrible first semester, but Pat challenged him to come daily for supper and study until midnight. He did this and improved his grades significantly, a challenge that was successful.

Altricia called in late January and was experiencing signs of pregnancy. Pat flew down and drove her back home. She lived with us until the following year. Her daughter was born on Tuesday, September 17th, our first grandchild. Altricia returned to SC State in January of 1992. She took her daughter, Alyssa with her. We really missed her and the baby, but realized it was best for the both of them.

I continued to pastor St. John, but felt terrible that my house was not in order. My daughter was a single mother and my son had run away from home, claiming that he wanted to live in "the hood." We lived in a "glass house" so he thought, and he was not comfortable living with us. This really hurt. The only thing I had going for me was my best friend and wife, Pat. We walked three miles, Monday through Friday, at five in the morning. We meditated for the first mile and a half. Then we would talk about our day that lay ahead. Pat was very supportive of my research agendas. We also did much research together and published. We spent time during our morning walks and lunch breaks discussing the obstacles and pitfalls we were facing in our lives, personally and professionally.

St. John continued to be a stronghold and support mechanism for us in many ways. I was very involved on the Tenth District level. I chaired the Examiner's Board of our conference and the Trustee Board. It was very time consuming, yet very fulfilling. I felt appreciated and loved by most members of the congregation. In the late nineties, I was appointed to the Trustee Board of Paul Quinn College, an AME school and a historically Black university. I served on this board for several years,

In the fall of 1995, I received a call from the dean's office about my promotion packet. This was for full professor. I approached my department head and he said he hadn't told me because he didn't think I was ready for promotion. I was very hurt by his remarks and talked to several of my colleagues. They encouraged me to submit the packet. I was given the packet back twice and told that it lacked this or that. I was given the packet back the day before it was due in the dean's office. I was leaving town the next morning to handle some business with my daughter in South Carolina. I took the packet and made the recommended corrections that night at Wash's house and left it on the desk of Debbie King, the administrative assistant. I called her from a pay phone while en route to the airport. She informed me that she had received it, completed it, and was getting ready to send it over. I was elated for her untimely work on the behalf of so many, but this time, on my behalf. I received full support from the departmental faculty, but my department head's letter still haunts me.

It read, "I recommend Dr. Larke with reservations...." It concluded with the same.

The College and University committee voted in my favor, and in March of 1996 I received confirmation that the Board of Regents had promoted me to the rank of Full Professor.

That fall as I contemplated my future, I was in deep thought about what was next. I had become the first African American to move from Assistant Professor to Full Professor in the one-hundred-year history of Texas A&M University. I recall my first day of the fall semester, Dr. Gary Briers escorted me and my teaching assistant to my class. He said he had an announcement to make. He stood and introduced me as the first African American to reach the pinnacle of full professor. The class applauded, and because of my not liking or appreciating celebrations, I continued with my prepared lecture.

Seeking other opportunities, I was told about the American Council of Education (ACE) Fellowship program. The application was quite rigorous, yet I was encouraged by several people to give it a try. I flew to Washington, DC for a two day interview. The following week I received a letter of congratulations. I accepted it and made reservations for the orientation.

The orientation went well and I was accepted in to the ACE program. I was excited about the new challenge. I now had to find a place to do a year-long internship with a president of a college or university. This would require me to take leave of my teaching and leadership roles in my department. The worse part, of course, was the doctoral students I was currently chairing. With that in mind, I looked closely at Baylor. This would allow me to continue mentoring my doctoral and master's students. This would also allow me the privilege of remaining in the pulpit of St. John.

I had an interview with Dr. Sloan, President, and Dr. Smetlekopft, of the Chief Academic Affairs Office. Almost immediately, I was asked to come on as Executive Assistant to President Sloan. They would provide an apartment on or close to campus. I looked at several that afternoon and selected one close to campus, and begin moving there that weekend.

I began my internship there in the fall semester of 1997. I served on several committees at the University. The Athletic Council provided knowledge on rules and regulations for athletes. It was time-consuming, but very rewarding. I learned a great deal about the student athletes and the expectations. My son, Aaron, and I traveled quite a bit with the Council, since Pat was always at some meeting or had other interests.

My tenure at A&M continued to be fruitful for me and many students. I have always considered myself to be an advocate for students. Especially those students, whom others had counted out. With proper mentoring, any student can reach his or her potential. During that time at A&M, I chaired, co-chaired or was a member of over 300 doctoral and master student committees. I still remain in touch with many of them.

One of my graduate students encouraged me to consider a study abroad. I did all the paperwork and was approved for a study abroad in 2011 until 2014. It was very informative. We took forty students and several faculty members to Brazil, South America. David DeSousa assisted with the trip and was our interpreter. The culture was very challenging. The language barrier was real, but David, my teaching assistant helped tremendously since he was a native Brazillian. We had a very enjoyable experience since Pat was able to attend.

On July 17, 2014, I retired from the prestigious Texas A&M University, College Station, Texas, and received Professor Emeritus, and the rest is history.

I look back and wonder, "How I made it over!"

THIS BATTLE OF THE MINISTRY

It was indeed a battle, mostly internal. I asked myself questions concerning what others thought about my love for dancing and playing cards. Surely, preachers didn't do those things. At least, I didn't know if Reverends Naaman Bryant, Boston, Seward, and Harris couldn't or didn't do those things. People seemed to love them, but I just couldn't take the chance not being happy in this life. I failed to accept my "calling" sooner but rather later.

I bargained with the Lord. "Lord, if you permit me to obtain my doctorate degree, then I will answer your call." He called as early as my pre-teens. It wasn't until September 19, 1982, that I surrendered, and a burden was lifted. I accepted my call to the ministry under Rev. Paul Harris, at St. Paul AME Church, Columbia, MO.

I began my ministerial classes immediately and traveled to St. Louis, Missouri, on the weekends. I was admitted in the fall of 1982. They moved Rev. Harris that year and along came Rev. Scott. He received me well and allowed me to preach often from his pulpit. I remained at St. Paul until departing and accepting a position at Texas A&M University in the summer of 1984. I left the 5th Episcopal and was transferred to the 10th Episcopal District.

My family and I joined Allen Chapel AME Church under the leadership of Rev. B.T. Langham. I was admitted to the Texas Conference and ordained an itinerant deacon in September of 1984. Almost immediately, I was assigned a small church in Calvert, TX: this was my first church, St. James AME Church. It held services on first and third Sundays and this allowed us to continue worshipping at Allen Chapel on the other Sundays.

St. James was a small frame church with no water, only electricity and a piano with minimal keys. My wife and I quickly purchased a piano for the church. The congregation consisted of seven senior citizens, all females. Only four of them were able to physically attend services. First, we had to establish a checking account. They kept their money in a member's home. They were very reluctant to obtain a checking account. They had little trust in the financial institutions. After several meetings, I persuaded them and took two of the members with me to the bank. The two of them cashed their checks there but didn't have an account there. It was Citizen's Bank and Trust. I didn't want my name on the checks so encouraged them to place their names on the account. They were very proud as they returned to their homes with the privilege of signing a check.

I was ordained an itinerant elder in AME Church in September of 1986. That gave me the ability to perform all services, including consecrating the communion elements. That was an asset because I had asked Rev. Langham to consecrate the elements for services prior to receiving the final ordination.

I was given an additional church in 1986, Bethel AME Church in Hearne, Texas. It met every Sunday, so I would go there then leave and go to Calvert on first and third Sundays. This took me away from Allen Chapel. I loved the people at Allen Chapel and was called to do several funerals for their loved ones.

My ministry prospered by leaps and bounds during the three years at Calvert. The congregation grew rapidly. We had grown to a membership of thirty-five, mostly youngsters. However, that success led to being promoted in the AME Church. A friend of mine called and asked me to consider a church in Brenham. Pat and I drove over for their Annual Conference. We discussed the pros and cons of a move. At the Houston Annual Conference, in September of 1987, I was called in to meet with Bishop Rembert Stokes. He asked me to accept St. John in Brenham, building me up by telling me how much I had accomplished. He wanted to promote me and said that I would be an asset to St. John and the West Texas Conference. I told him, I didn't want the challenge.

He responded, "Are you Baptist or Methodist?"

I responded, "Methodist."

His response haunted me for years. He said, "I am sending you."

Each time, I encountered the least problem, I would hear those words, "I am sending you."

We were told to prepare bulletins for sixty-six, and we never had sixty-six worshippers. It was always more. We were loved by most of the parishioners, but a few let it be known that they were not pleased with my youthfulness and made it very difficult for me. I was overwhelmingly loved by the conference and was immediately placed on many of the boards. This included chairing the Examiner's Board. This was great for me, because I enjoyed teaching.

General Conferences in the AME Church are held every four years. I was elected a delegate to the conference in 1992, 1996, 2000, 2004, 2008, 2012 and 2016. I was appointed to the Board of

Trustees of Paul Quinn College in Dallas, Texas and remained on that Board for several years.

During my tenure at St. John, a lot happened. Many deaths and funerals. Two of them were my mother in October 2000 and my father in February 2016. My prayer the whole time I was away was to never receive a call that either of my parents had passed. God granted my request. My mom went in the hospital on July 21st and passed away on Saturday, October 7, 2000. It was a difficult time for me. I was asked by my siblings to do the eulogy. I assured them I would, on one condition, they hold their emotions during the services. It went well. This was indeed a difficult moment. I felt lost. I used the scripture, Proverbs 31:10, for her services. My siblings did as they promised, and the funeral went well. My mom was now gone. The family has never been the same. My daddy seemed to get along fine. It was not the case for me. He assured me, "She isn't coming back." I reminded him of how he grieved over his mother's death. I was nine when she passed, but remember how he grieved openly. We agreed to differ. My daddy quickly started dating but it was too quick for most of us. I shared with him my disappointment and he repeated the phrase, "your moma is not coming back." We differ on the timing. It was quick, less than a week. He never spent a night away from home.

In 2005, I received a call that my sister, Ruth Elaine, had located my Dad and would drive down from Wake Forest, North Carolina to meet my Dad. Daddy had father her while he was a serviceman in Virginia. Moma knew about Elaine and had a picture sent to Daddy when Elaine was very young. Elaine and I are four-and-one-half months apart, agewise. I eulogized Elaine's mother in 2012.

On February 1, 2016, my daddy passed away. I had come to South Carolina that weekend to attend Mr. Boston Johnson's wife's funeral. I had planned to spend a week visiting in South Carolina. I was scheduled to spend Monday and part of Tuesday with Daddy. He had not eaten any breakfast and said he did not want any breakfast. My brother, Warren came by that morning. Daddy began breathing with some difficulty. I stood up and asked him if he was okay and if he was angry with anyone. He replied, "No." So, I said you can go now. He passed away just like that, and I summoned the nursing staff. They dismissed me from the room, and I called my siblings. We said our goodbye and watched till the morticians arrived. We said farewell to our 93-year-old patriarch.

THE LATTER DAYS...

We always wanted to retire to South Carolina. When we started approaching retirement, we put some plans in motion. After my retirement from Texas A&M University in July of 2014, we began the search for housing in South Carolina. After Daddy's death in February of 2016, we agreed to buy the homestead but that didn't happen. My brother, Charles, the executor of Daddy's will, said the will stated the house would not be sold.

In May of 2016, we flew to South Carolina to eulogize a first cousin and to perform Perry Jones and Delphine Warren's wedding. I taught Perry in high school and he was also, Wash's brother. It was a busy Memorial Day weekend. My wife received a call from a relative who was a realtor. We rode down Pine Log Road and the house that I passed when I was bussed in high school was for sale. I never looked at this home because it was a plantation home, and that carried a stigma of slavery.

We passed this house several times and finally the GPS noted that we were in front of the destination. We drove up and Pat, of course, immediately took a liking to it and asked if we could see it. Nancy, the realtor, agreed to show it to us that Monday afternoon.

We liked it and were tickled that it had 11.95 acres of land, including a pecan orchard. It was a dream in the making. I visualized my chickens, ducks, and guineas in the backyard. A garden of fresh vegetables. It appeared to be more house than we needed, but we would see. We left a check with my sister, Emma, for the realtor. We returned to Texas on Tuesday, May 31st, and received the call that we had been approved for a home loan.

We had already made plans to vacation in Costa Rica in July, so we were unable to appear for the closing scheduled for July 27th, 2016. We asked my brother, Charles, and my sister, Emma, to represent us. Everything went as planned and we became homeowners in the state of South Carolina.

Pat and Altricia flew back from Costa Rica and placed a mailbox on the property. We were given the address of 772 Pine Log Road, Beech Island. We made preparations for Tricia to move into the home as we finished our time in Texas. Pat would retire from Texas A&M University and I would complete my thirtieth year at St. John AME Church.

We flew back several times and made additions and renovations of flooring and paint colors to resemble the home we had inhabited in College Station. We also converted a workshop into a two-car a garage, added a fireplace in the family room.

I announced my resignation from St. John AME Church in March of 2017. They made plans for my retirement, and it included a musical. It was planned for late August to coincide with Pat's retirement from the university. That weekend, a hurricane came through and the church musical was canceled. The retirement for Pat was held as planned and was well-attended by many.

We begin making arrangements for the move to South Carolina. Getting the vehicles to South Carolina was planned to coincide with Calvin, Marilyn, Perry and Delphine coming to the retirement ceremonies. They would fly out and drive the vehicles back to South Carolina. So, Calvin and Marilyn drove the Mercedes and Perry and Marilyn drove the Toyota pickup back to South Carolina.

I begin to wrap up my tenure at St. John, which included an audit of the books. I had been there for thirty years and had the longest tenure in the history of that church. I had the second longest on record in Texas following Rev. E.E. Coates who pastored more than thirty years at Wesley AME Church in Houston, Texas. I preached my final sermon there on Sunday, October 8, 2017. It was a packed church with many of my A&M colleagues in attendance. I selected Numbers 13:26-30 as text and the subject, "We Can Overcome." Talking about the giants and the grasshoppers. Many tears flowed that day, mine included, as I stood there as pastor for the final time. Whatever is before you, jut know that it's small when you put God first. Problems become small when we place them in His hands. I momentarily thought of the many baptisms, weddings and funerals performed during my thirty-year tenure. Bittersweet moments.

Pat and I left for the Southwest Annual Conference to be held in San Antonio, TX. We made our final report on Thursday, October 12th. We received a standing ovation as we departed the Immanuel AME Church Sanctuary. Many of St. John's members bade us farewell as we drove away. We arrived at Wash's house that afternoon and departed early the next morning with our belongings. Aaron had our dog, Lucky, in a crate on the back of his truck. Della, Glenn, Pat, and I rode in the Tahoe. That was Friday the 13th, but we arrived intact late that afternoon. Jay, our grandson who lived with us in South Carolina, had moved here during the late August and was attending Midland Valley High School.

The first Sunday here, we visited my home church, St. Catherine CME Church. The fourth Sunday, we visited the Runs Missionary Baptist Church and Cumberland AME Church. The first Sunday in November, we attended Cumberland and were invited to the District's Post planning meeting in Florence. It was here that Bishop Green assigned me to the pastorage of Cumberland AME Church, AIKEN.

Retirement from the ministry was not final. My first sermon at Cumberland was delivered on Sunday, November 12, 2017. The scripture, Matthew 21:42b, and the subject, "This Is the Lord's Doing!" I again began mentoring younger clergy in the ministry. We were well-received by the congregation.

All of us are now in our respective places. Aaron is with the junior Sunday school class, junior usher board, and youth choir. Altricia is with the young people's department and the missionary department. Pat is a Life Member of the Missionary Society and serves as advisor to the local society.

I have joined the Omicron Tau Lambda Chapter of Alpha Phi Alpha Fraternity and serve as the Chapter's Chaplain.

The Local Chapter of the National Association for the Advancement of Colored People (NAACP)

Active with the Jefferson High School Class of 1964.

Active member of SCSU Alumni Association, Augusta Chapter.

I serve as Founding Board Member of the Promised Land Families Ministry (PLFM), Gainesville, Florida.

Several Prayer Ministries to include Sweet Canaan, Piedmont, SC; Bible Way - Atlas Road, Columbia, SC; Bible Way Christian Fellowship- Baltimore, MD and Mt. Pleasant, Jackson, SC.

Currently Serving as Supply Pastor, St. Paul AME Church, Abbeville, SC.

I am trying very hard to fulfill Boston Johnson's legacy of mentoring those who others have given up on!

ABOUT THE AUTHOR

Rev. Dr. Alvin Larke's, a native South Carolinian, received his B.S. degree in Agricultural Education from SC State College (now University) and a Master's of Education from the same specializing in Special Education. He did further studies at the University of South Carolina and Clemson University. Alvin taught vocational agriculture for 12 years in Calhoun County (South Carolina). He received his Ph. D in Agricultural Education from the University of Missouri-Columbia. In 1984, he accepted a position at Texas A&M University; he retired as a full professor in 2014. Alvin is an ordained AME minister. He pastored for over 38 years in Texas.

REV. DR. ALVIN LARKE'S PROFESSIONAL

EXPERIENCES INCLUDED:

American Council on Education (ACE) Fellow

Special Assistant to the Executive Vice President and Provost

Director of Ag Jumpstart Program

Coordinator of the of Agricultural Development Program

Coordinator of Agricultural Science Program

Coordinator of the Graduate Program, Department Agricultural

Leadership and Communications

President of the African American Professional Organization

I served on the following committees or initiatives:

Scholarship Committee, College of Agriculture and Life Sciences

Race and Ethnic Studies Institute Internal Advisory Council

Council on Teacher Education

University Athletic Council

Faculty Senate (two three year terms)

President's Task Force to Evaluate U.S. Cultures and International

Requirements Proposal

Chair, Admissions Sub-Committee, Athletic Council

Chair, Graduate Minority Fellowship Committee

Search Advisory Committee for Head of Department of

Agricultural Education, 1984 and 1993.

Committee for Restructuring the College of Education

Co-Chair, Faculty Senate, Senate Minority Conditions

Subcommittee

Search Advisory Committee, Director, Student Diversity Office,

College of Agriculture and Life Sciences

University Appeals Committee Panel

Courses Taught:

Undergraduate;

Introduction to Agricultural Education

Course Building

Methods in Adult Agricultural Education

Student Teaching in Agricultural Education

Principles of Technological Change

Agricultural Extension Organization and Methods

Cultural Pluralism in Agriculture

Introduction to Agricultural Science Teaching

Graduate Courses:

Principles of Adult Education

Workshop in Agricultural Education

Methods of Technological Change

Philosophy of Agricultural Education

Guidance and Counseling of Rural Youth

Transfer of Technology by Institutions

Developed and Taught:

Introduction of Agricultural Science Teaching (AGSC 301)

Cultural Pluralism in Agriculture (ALED 422)

AWARDS AND HONORS

American Council on Education Fellow

Distinguished Teaching Award, American Association for
Agricultural Education

Distinguished Service Award, American Association for
Agricultural Education

Professor, Summer Scholar's Program, Penn State University

T Camp named in my Honor

Fish Camp named in the Larke's Honor

Elected to Alpha Zeta, Gamma Sigma Delta, and Phi Delta Kappa

Elected as a George Washington Carver Fellow

Chair of Institutional Review Board (IRB)

Invited Participant, The Oxford Roundtable, Diversity In Society, Oxford, England. Pat was able to accompany me on that experience.

Served as President of the National Society for Minorities in Agricultural, Natural Resources and Related Sciences (MANNRS), 2005-2006.

www.ingramcontent.com/pod-product-compliance
Lightning Source LLC
Chambersburg PA
CBHW051323120626
46547CB00015B/2364

* 9 7 9 8 9 8 6 8 6 2 0 8 8 *